THE HAUNT OF TIME

Chosen Poems, Old and New

Henry Chapin

Introduction by
Josephine Jacobsen

William L. Bauhan, Publisher
DUBLIN, NEW HAMPSHIRE

Library of Congress Cataloging in Publication Data

Chapin, Henry, 1893-
The Haunt of Time.
I. Title.
PS3505.H3514.A17 1981 811'.52 81-8103
ISBN 0-87233-056-7 AACR2

Some of the poems in this book have previously appeared in *The London Mercury, The Review of Literature, The Sound, The Berkshire Eagle,* and *New Letters,* as well as in the author's earlier books of poems: *Leifsaga,* 1934; *West Walking Yankee,* 1940; *To the End of West,* 1970; *A Celebration,* 1974; and *The Constant God,* 1978.

PRINTED IN THE UNITED STATES OF AMERICA

P.P.C.

The author is profoundly grateful to Penney Chapin Hills for the precise job of editing — and the deep understanding — she has contributed to this work.

H.C.

Contents

II. Variable Music

III. The Haunt of Time

IV. American

Introduction

IT IS A FAIR GENERALIZATION to say that, in 1981, there is more poetry, bad and good, being written in the United States than at any previous period. Its shape is not definitive—far more range in form and technique is accepted than was the case even five years ago, a period when traditional forms had come to be regarded as a sort of obsolescent aberration. As always, the good poetry is smaller in bulk than the bad; as always, truly distinguished poetry is rarest of all. The amount of junk is dismal; what is encouraging is the variety of the distinguished work.

In this last rare category exists both the poetry which concerns itself directly with the problems, motions and controversies of specifically contemporary life, and the poetry which, with classic stubbornness, concerns itself primarily with the roots of humanity and the natural world; with the perennial emotions; with the fate that has been confronted by human beings down through the centuries. Henry Chapin's poetry belongs with the latter group.

When this sort of poetry is written by a fine poet, there is about it an ageless quality, a direct thrust to the basic emotions. It has the austere durability of rock, and the freshness of new growth. As early as 1926, Chapin was publishing poetry in the *London Mercury* along with John Masefield, Siegfried Sassoon and William Butler Yeats. Now this book, his chosen poems, old and new, brings together earlier poems from *A Celebration,* more recent work from *The Constant God,* a few selections from the two long narrative works, and a number of new poems; it gives, in depth and range, the essence of his particular gifts of strength and invincible freshness. It is the work of an intellectual man of no patience with the evasive or obscure, a man with a boundless curiosity, and a lyricism which is neither thin nor lush. The sexuality of the work is strong, and too sure of itself to be declamatory.

Whatever Chapin sees, he sees head-on, whether the *leather lips curly beard, shaggy flanks uprearing/ and the old, cold topaz/ of a billy-goat's eye* . . . or, flicking through branches, *red squirrels/ propelled by their curses* . . . or midnight mice: *when the moon slides over the floor,/ slick as thought/ they whisk into a dance/ mad with minute joys* . . . But, as in any poetry worth reading, the human encounter with pain, loss, renewal, death and love, is always in the air.

Though Chapin has lived and written in London and in Paris, it is New England which is the poetry's root, and there is a strong drawing toward the sea, a sea precious because unfenced, unplowed, untameable. *There is no ocean conquest, save by art.*

The artist's question here is always, What next? *Mud underfoot, the slash of wilderness/ serpents draining across his path/ voices proclaiming doom, only excite/ his childish wonder. Make way. Let him pass.* The long elegiac love poem, *I Beg To Report* is admirably sustained. I can think of no poem celebrating the difficult span of mature love as close to the quality of William Carlos Williams's *Asphodel, That Greeny Flower.*

There is a tough, tall, breezy irony in much of the work: courage is everywhere implicit. It is understood that joy—abundant in the poems—cannot be facile; "joy," he says, "is the gift of courage."

His special star is not available to astronauts. Watching it at four A.M.: *Let me warn you/ man is a spoiler./ In terror he plunders/ in panic he slays./ If you dare, come swiftly/ and soon to our aid./ Never mind wonders/ loving kindness will do./ I hold your bright image fast in my sight./ If you're ready, I'm ready/ Try me some night.*

Chapin is no optimist; it is simply that he finds life irresistibly desirable; constantly he returns to . . . *self-renewing roots of joy/ where the heart's gladness lives.*

He is incurably American. Without a line of patriotic rhetoric, deeply and inevitably his poetry rises out of New England. Greece is there, the old sagas and myths are there, but the strength and sap are fed from the New England soil. Helios, Hylas, all the powers of spring, translate themselves into New England heat or chill or smells or sounds.

At just this point in the development of American poetry, that of Henry Chapin has a special value. It runs as a living linkage, traditional in its roots and their expression, creative in its vitality, its freedom from cliché and sham. Spanning more than half a century, it is an extraordinary amalgam of gusto, lyricism, irony and self-awareness. *Irony is the joke we share with God/ crying: Father, how deftly/ you pull out the rug.* This sustained accomplishment is rare, and it deserves the widest sort of recognition. If one bewares of calling it unique, certainly it is special and heartening. Life does not seem to have explained to Henry Chapin about the diminishing returns of creativity in old age. It is *Nobody Listens,* all over again:

> I bring home the saplings
> fresh-cut, thrust them into earth
> for the planting of beans,
> to climb, flower, hang ripe.
>
> I come to the spring-garden
> beans in hand. What do I see?
> Green ears sprout from the saplings,
> I forgot to tell them.

JOSEPHINE JACOBSEN

Baltimore, Maryland
May 1981

I

Horizons

Li Po Comes Home

He packs his pony,
ink, plumes, paper
and other paraphernalia.
He sets off for the mountain
done with the court.
Long days pass
under hills and the tented sky.
He dismounts at his hut.

The sun slides down the west.
He sits above the village
refreshed by the sound of waters.
Fingers of the pine fracture the moon.
Work done at the end of day,
laughter sweeps up from the women
who splash in the village pool.
From the palm of night
stars speak for silence.
Only the nightingale sings.

Li Po inscribes a poem,
just so they will know,
He pins it on a reed
and that to a floating chip,
watching as it turns and twists
beyond the trees into the pool.

Suddenly the laughter is broken,
then rises with glee.
Presently small feet mount the path.
Smiling askance, she bows to the master.

In the girl's arms a napkin,
in the napkin a supper for two.

As she bends to the fire
Li Po reaches for the wine.
She spreads a cloth at his feet.
The cup passes. They sup and sing.
His round belly catches the moon.
His eyes are pools of pleasure.

A cool breath falls from the mountain.
Li Po opens his robe of fur.
Smiling, she slides in.
Li Po dismisses the moon.

Morning Song

Tis prime of day. I've snored away the night.
No fault of mine white gosmer decks the hedge
or silvery dew refreshes tired sward.
Someone set it going, wound-up small fowl
to loop the airs, mad with exuberance,
swaying the lovely tree-tops with their song.
Mockers mock on, erupting in pure joy
from yon green fountains. A-field the bob-whites
with sweet deliberation pipe the dawn,-
witless creatures who seem to feel this earth
a dish of wonders for their pure delight.
I recall, once upon a time, long gone,
man too awakened Eden with full song.

Gulls

Wherever I am I see them
on sliding wing in the windy places,
scattering their sharp cries, veering
up the invisible stairways,
lost in brightness of that other blue
whereunder spreads the carven sea
whose surges stitch white land-seam.

Wherever I am, the thin crying,
the jeering cackle, the insane
salt mockery, calls to my ghost;
unfetters the cold, the impersonal
daemon whose winnowing pinions
shake off spell of familiar earth
and all the haunting hearthside names.

When evening gathers under the hill,
lanterns glint above the waters,
and the land bells are tolling;
my own and those others fare away,
wing-tip, wave-tip shadow meeting,
til all the sound in a world of silence
is the thunder and the hush and thunder
voice of ocean.

Ballade of Spring

Drugged with weight of winter woe
on a bank of last year's hay
I lay my weary bones, just so,
and stare into the vacant day,
my eyes seeking the wide ocean
of sweeping sky, where God Apollo
draws up red sap, floods the hollow
galleries of New England brain
with blind sensations lustful pain,
indeed, with many a sinful notion,
while secretly from toe to crown
the crimson freshets start and run,
thawing in the sun hum-a-hum.

Yon bird who rolls around the sky
sees something coming more than I.
O, sun-bedrunken, tell me true
what I lack that's clear to you
up the zenith's winding stair
with wide horizons in your eye?
"I see," he said, "I see, I spy
in the southlands far and far,
dancing and laughing in the sun
a flood that keeps a coming on.
The April ocean wide and green
is pressing on the shores of March,
quick as flame that licks the drouth
small grass comes leaping from the south."
"I hear," he whispered, "think I hear
waves of bird-song drawing near.
Oh, bright and silver sounding stream

from bluebird and the whippoorwill
and little peepers that cry so shrill."

He left me silent down below
sensing with hand against the sod
the slow, oncoming tread of God:
the earthworm winding underfoot,
the grubbing mole, the pushing root;
my ear pressed gently on the trees
listening, listening for the flood
of the forest's crystal blood
where fountain-wells of sap unfreeze.

The lurching plow has turned the mold
with many a shining fold on fold
of steaming earth. Now I smell
arbutus under woodland eaves
and violets folded in the dell,
all the flower-laden breeze.
The yellowhammer's frenzied bill
waking echoes from the hill,
chipmunk chattering on the wall,
the old black crow's familiar call
where he labors through the air.
These things I see, I smell, I hear
before true spring has come to town,
about the time of blossoms snowing.
Green tide of small grass leaping,
with frosty froth of bluets sweeping,
breeds a music in my heart,
a secret river of laughter,
when wading in fresh waves of verdure
the sun-mad heifers mill and run
as the bull comes down the pasture.

Nobody Listens

I bring home the saplings
fresh-cut, thrust them into earth
for the planting of beans,
to climb, flower, hang ripe.

I come to the spring-garden
beans in hand. What do I see?
Green ears sprout from the saplings.
I forgot to tell them.

New England Sentiment

When I am asked: Where is your home,
what country do you call your own?
New England answers from my lips
and like a fountain-wingéd lark
fills the spaces of my heart.
For there was I begot and bred,
there my fathers were before me,
ten generations of men,
Huguenots from France,
farmers in England,
breakers of the Bay Path.
Backs turned from bigotry,
they came to dwell by the blue hills
east of the river Connecticut,
where the hundredth mile of forest trail
breaks to the plain from Chicopee.

There by the river they came to rest
and the stroke of their axes
when they built their cabins
will echo in the ears of their sons forever.
I know the cabins in a row
and their evening smoke so still,
and the whip-poor-will in the dusk
by the whispering walls of forest;
and the prayerful pioneers,
as clear men studying plainness,
who were not too curious
of the human mysteries
nor yet purchasers of grace.
Free men who found no time to dwell

on the glories of their fathers
and free because they would not hoard
for the safety of their sons.

Oh, fortunate,
with heart and mind set free
from the traffic of thronged places;
who strode with the knowledge of good
into the wide wilderness,
and stubbornly there,
as with one heart, hand and shoulder,
brought great matters to pass,
confident for their well-begotten
more light would break from the word of God
than they were yet aware.

Now still where our fathers built
white villages by streams, and elms
pattern the meadowlands
with feathery fountains green,
deep in the hills and valleys
the eternal sources flow.

There by the slow Housatonic
and the Berkshire hills above,
the ranging seasons blow and pass
weaving their patterns on rock and grass
with the rough hands of love.
Summer's brassy sun beats down,
the quivering forest leaves are hushed,
brooding thunders roll from the mountain
with stalking fire.

Once more the leaping brooks
are loud in the dusk.

The slow stars burn
and the lilac bush by the door
shakes down her odorous dew.

The scarlet hills of fall
fill with the clatter of reaping.
Barnyard axemen hew and fling
the snowy birch in drifts so fragrant,
thinking of winter.

One soft April night
the erstwhile silent marshes
ring aloud with elfin pipings
of Hylas, that bubbly atomy
whose sweet throat heralds spring;
and now, by the wood's edge
caging under last year's leaves
her delicate swooning breath,
blooms the arbutus,
of all flowers the flower.

My heart was great with awe
when slow pacing at the fall of night
I stood in the golden valley
filled with the gathering might
of the mountain, and saw
eternity as in a dream,
through the meadow grasses
and the flower drifted plain.

Now in the bright familiar dawn
I gather my ghost in my breast.
Who can desire more content
than to tread and cherish;

delighting in those springs
whereby his own people
have long been nourished,
earning their right
and their portion in Jerusalem.

Why Not?

Today I heard the homing of the geese,
free within rhythms they were unaware,
wavering high above the salty marsh.
On a surf of wing the wild swans rise,
their long necks penetrate the empty skies,
their fierce pinions menacing the air.
Of what concern the measure of our day
if life can thus take off and wing away?

Mike from Finland

That's all it says
on this square stone
in this Yankee graveyard;
Mike from Finland.
What more to know?
Old, lost, young, desperate
or traveller well-content?

Here it's as near to Where
as anywhere. The eternal
question never answered.
But this we do know.
Mike had friends
to raise up this small stone
in this home port
and say, at least, where from
and name his name.

Let the old forefathers,
snug under their wolf-stones
tell him, if they can,
what more.

Horizon Breaker

After the dull hours of school,
remember the boy who ran,
who hid his books beneath the porch,
ran through the back yards,
shinnied the high fences
and crossed the sand-lots to the railroad track?

What is it you catch, boy,
with your ear pressed to the earth?
Is the hard earth tremulous,
alive to far off excitements,
is something pent-up about to break?
Hark! The distant muttering and rumble,
the fantastical oncoming dancer.
What does your cocked ear
strain from the eastern breeze?
Faint wail, gusty transcendent shriek —
what monster with galumphing gallop,
free-moving like the whirlwind,
crashes nearer and nearer upon you?
Shade your eyes, boy,
Far down the glistening roadbed
where ribbons of steel become one point,
that point enlarges bigger and bigger.

Hold your ground, boy,
See how she sways, lurching and leaping
instant by instant hurtling nearer.
Hold fast, the well-spiked tracks are sure.
The shrill complaining cars are by:
only the dust whirls down the roadbed.

There are people in those window flashes
who will think about you for miles and miles,
as the boy with the big eyes and gaping mouth
who drowned himself in unholy terror,
who cleansed his soul and sucked strange power,
sensing the mystery that dwells beyond
his own familiar street. And what grandeur
if only for that moment, to worship
this steam-exhaling, fire-drunken slave.
How good for tired voyagers in cars
to catch their breath, beholding the image
of the incomparable horizon-breaker,
this magnificent runner, reflected
in the clear eyes of undefeated boy.

One day, remember, I said to myself:
Come now, pack your duds, let's beat it.
Just climb aboard with a long blue ticket,
lope down into a seat and wait
while the delicate-stepping beast
eases backward with immense restraint,
couples, clinches and shakes alive the train.
All aboard and goodbye people.
Others, myself all here suspended.
Hours of departure are nothingness,
only a void of inattentive hearts
impatient for release. Slowly glide
imperceptibly out of each other's
existence. What a relief for us all.
Lickity-clickity, lickity-clickity —
cast off, cast off, forget them every one.

I had never ridden the through express
non-stop, with all-steel sleeping cars attached.
Come now, I thought

death might come to feel like this,
casual and unceremonious,
holding the heart suspended
for imminent excitements vast and strange.
This is something like, something kinglike,
a most worthy crowning of existence.
This whole wide world of circling hills and trees
whirling near-to and marching far away —
most beautiful maneuvers, excellent.
Quick change of scene, diverting incidents,
the sharp surprise of uncurtained windows,
naked frogs of boys in the silver streams,
lovers loosing themselves in the thickets —
Better by far than the world unmoving
and me on shank's mare snuffing the dust,
turned to a roadside curser of traffic.

He couldn't whirl this show too fast for me;
couldn't play tunes for my unusened ear
sweeter than steel wheel glancing over steel,
the sorrowful murmur of crossing bells,
the whoop-la of the engine in the hills.

We drag behind the slow sun, drag before
the easy flooding darkness. The red ball
slides behind the fire-tipped mountains.
Large night bends low and shakes her glistening mane.
Pull tight all blinds. Let's gaze on homely things,
forget the sudden menace, demon blast,
the glare and panic of the passing trains
caught out and tearing homeward through the dark.
Crawl into bed, curl up and make a ball
close prisoned in these shooting walls of steel.
Then from this cell one final searching glance
where overhead the heavens themselves careen.

And last of all, seek out those giant few
which for their brightness conquer the world's edge,
threading the branchy night.
Floating down the silver rails of night, no,
sable wings, no, silver rails that sweep
upward through starry pastures and across
the topmost peaks of heaven. Pray regard
those whirling balls, each with its little moon,
spheres that spin a wiry kind of music
mixed with sounds of voices, of bells that drift
upon the humming gales. Pray regard
the lovely glow of earth-shine far beneath,
silver seas and yellow sands rolling
like Dolphin through the oceans of the air,
where people sleep in shadow, stir in sun,
unwitting of these star-infested heights
where, homelike as a comet on its course,
we sing along.

I arise into the prime of morning,
step briskly down, where the expectant eyes
want to know,
what contraband from other side of darkness
has come a-trundling with us all night long.

My Father

I took my father for granted,
never thought him courageous,
A clean watchful man
who never raised his voice;
never stood at a barricade
but quietly held his course.
Never unjust to the young,
never betrayed his trust.
Secret in his love.

Now I know
the small disciplines of day by day,
spoke for a valiant heart.

Adam's First Glance

There was plenty of light when I went walking,
spires of brown and gold all in company.
Why, I'll call them ferns, said I, as they moved
dancing along to invisible music.
Says I: This is wind. That hand on my cheek
I will likewise claim, so let it be air.
It hastens the red blood through the body,
sweet in the lungs, a word on the tongue.

So be, I cried: Body, muscle, sleek of skin.
I leapt with delight. A ball of splendor
walked the sky. Sun, sky, wind and word, all;
the moon in its seasons, the stream that sings,
the shade of woods, all native to my tongue,
(first glance, first breath, first healing warmth of sun.)
No questions asked; companions to my wonder.
Come what may, am I not then co-author
for everlasting with God Helios
of my own life? I named it. I have it.

Dowser

I plucked the wishbone from my breast
shaping a dowser wand.
I honed it sharp and clean,
that it again reveal the heart,
give answer to delight.

I sought the upland pasture
I knew from other days,
waiting for the pull and tug
where joy had drained from sight.

I had to believe there must be
a secret spring survived,
where once familiar waters,
in anwer to my dowser wand
would rise again to life.

Goat

There wasn't any wind
but the thorn tree was rustling
and out of its dusty leaves
gazed a yellow eye;
leather lips, curly beard,
shaggy shanks up-rearing,
and the old, cold topaz
of a billy goat's eye.

What, thought I to myself
quite suddenly,
how can he relish
this bitter kind of provender,
plucking with his leather lips
aloft and alone?
How can such a wise,
such a human looking critter,
relish so heartily
this prickly, this bitter
thorny kind of diet
here aloft and alone?

How can he linger,
when down along the mountainside
the bells of the nannies
go tinkle through the grasses;
when all along the waterside
willing little nannies
are fattening on the grasses
of the brook-side dell?

Far from the mountainside
down where the waters curled
a shepherd blew his horn, -
a short, harsh blast
upon his reedy horn.
Twitch went the stubby tail
of coarse old billy goat.
Down he dropped from thorn tree
leaping down the hillside
to his nannies in the dell.

Ha, thought I,
there goes old billy goat,
shaggy shanks, leather lips
and cold yellow eye.
Jesu! I repeated to myself,
quite suddenly,
trying to remember:
It's funny how time passes.
I wonder if he was a goat
that just went by?

Little Diver

What did you find, little diver,
down and down in the half-light?

My dinner of weed I saw
and, in the corner of one eye,
a jaw. Upward I shot,
broke through mirror into sun
and on strong wing took-off.

And what now, little diver?

I'll dive and dive again
to pluck the delicate weed,
despite awaiting jaw.
Have I not web and wing
and knowledge of the sun?

Dolphin

What need of wings with such an arc of flight,
leaping from wave to wave. To man's despair
inheritors of grace and pure delight,
you sew your seam that binds the sea and air,
cruising in happy schools the gulfstream flood,
guest of the seasons, masters of your world,
where all lies open to your frolic mood,
as through the azure depths your bodies hurl.

If only sea-bound man had seen it through,
nor at creation struggled up the beach,
to fight forever for the joys that you,
Delphini, find so naturally in reach.
Good, pagan comrade, your inherent grace
and carefree ways confound the human race.

The Constant God
A Hymn

Shoot down your golden arrows, Helios,
upon your pensioner.
Draw the sea-mist, drink the dew
and light me on my way.
Paint green the brown,
then brown again the green,
'til fireflies, at dusk
spatter the heavy-headed wheat.
Lead us to harvest
in the whispering fields,
let morning flash the sickle blades
where golden armfuls fall to hand.
How rich and plentiful
the new trod grain
heaped on the threshing floor.
This harvest in, lead on
where heavy on the hillside
the ripe grapes hum with bees.
We'll fill the flowing vats,
spurt juice on naked thighs,
treading the golden and the crimson
blood of foison summer.
Now drink praise to Helios.

Let young bodies taste each other
as they tasted wine.
So evening falls,
the stewing pots are full.
New bread assails the nose,
the white cheese crumbles,
small orts from the mountains

and golden honey from the hollow trees,
stand by the well-mixed cup.
How delicate, Helios,
to draw the fragrant breath
as rosy dawn walks in
over the eastern sea.
My sleepy partner
yawns and rubs her eyes,
shakes out her tangled hair,
with slow smile invites
sport in the silver stream.
We rest on the thyme-sweet banks,
watching the flocks amble from fold.
Where simplicity spells plenty,
no greed lives,
no master wields a whip,
contentions die.
Helios, shine down upon our dance,
tuned to self-renewing roots of joy,
where the heart's gladness lives.

The Seventh Wave

The girls of summer skip and cry,
in and out with lunge of surf,
to tease.
                    But one fine day
they'll pause and plunge,
limbs flash through the combers,
hair careless on the wave.

Crepuscule

Dusk is the dangerous hour.
Man returns to his door
with fruits of the day.
A light in the house comes on.
There is sound of a voice,
a familiar face appears.
Try not to be alone when the sun goes down.

Fall

High geese echo
the hound in the wood,
The painted trees
are nervous with flocks.
Red squirrels,
propelled by their curses,
flick through the branches.
At the blue stab of a jay
more leaves idle to earth.
Bronze ferns give way
to the delicate drifting fox —
Wary, wary.
The dark pines wait.

Under the Eaves

At first hoar frost,
tunnels in mind
and a winter's nest,
beady-eyed, sly of foot
they slip in from the fields;
scouting about.

When the Big Cat stalks,
they drain in a trice
to attend on midnight and the moon.
Big ears, white bellies
and a switch of tail,
they scavenge where the giants supped,
for crumbs and delicates.

When moon slides over the floor,
slick as thought
they whisk into a dance,
mad with minute joys,
menace of the Cat to no avail.

Sensing the slit-eyed shadow
with dagger paw,
they flit to their tunnels
curling together in secret nests,
to dream of summer's lovelier quests.

Fieldings, lest it become too lonely,
erupt again upon the moonlit floor
and let your small ecstasies
shame with joy
poised evil of the Paw.

Winter Reverie

This hilltop burying ground is now disused.
Shoulder to shoulder the worn markers lean
casual to the last. In summer time
fringed gentian, wild flag and forget-me-not
conceal with stubborn grace each frosty name;
so winter with white cerements of snow.

Stranger, regard these dead only as names
life-graven by their holders and now fixed
in everlasting spirit; quiet dead,
who naturally, from brunt of battle,
at long last stumbled and their breathing stopped.

Take hold this stick. Carefully chip away
hood of last week's snow. This frosty stone
will show the name Marilla cleanly cut
beneath a willow's delicate drooping spray,
where floats a cherubim with wings for ears.
Marilla, who once dwelt upon that hill
in the white house, has long time come to be
this simple word, when locally uttered,
recalls beauty, character and spirit.
She was begot upon a winter's night
like this one, when the lash of crescent moon
was scarcely a pencil mark. Upon the hills
the intense grip of zero spread a charm
wherein the spears of starlight on the crust
glinted with a crisp visual music.

That summer was an easy breathing time.
Then sickle moon of Fall rode on above her.
Many a changing month of hot and cold
put forth their power, breeding up this tall;
gay-hearted creature, white-skinned, long of flank
whose supple form from easy moving hips
rose fountain-like and wayward on the stem.
Her voice picked up the quiet flowing stream,
her steady gaze a burning winter's blue.

Yonder village grows peaceful as this grave.
Sprinkled with hearth-fires the tide of dusk
floods up the eastern valley while the hills
show momentary gold of sunset farms.
Listen to the sleigh-bells, mark the clear sound
of Marilla, Marilla, Marilla.

Walk gently through this world of complete night
and harken for the whirling of the bells.
Gone. Not a bird to fill the empty air.
This winter stillness, like a quick shouting
or sudden fear, holds the caught listener.
Harken to the whirling of the sleigh-bells,
now brisk, now whispering they chime abroad.
Now they are gone. Drink in the burning air.
Shout! Echo slides away and then away.
There is a booming sound from Nine Mile pond;
nearby the trees tighten and crack with cold.
Stir and the frozen weeds crackle, as when
flame ravens the brittle of summer drouth.

Leave the shrill fox his frozen quest,
nothing is left but vain music of stars
a drifting summer gnat might hear, not I.
Go home. Time to wind the clock. Time to sleep.

This boozy, snow-bedrunken sense of peace,
bred of the zero air and silent night,
rings memory's knell. But hearken the faint sound
of Marilla, Marilla, Marilla.

Stranger waste no pity upon this grave.
Her life will echo in these hills when you
are dead. Her seed will thrive, when you are gone.

Chipmunk

Blessing or blast of sun,
kiss or the knife of wind,
chill hypnosis of the snow,
a stealthy wonder to begin.

Atomy, scamper along;
Tails-up explode from your wall.
Good things wait in the glade,
but, one eye to the tunnel
in your dark fort of rock.

You are nothing but a mouthful.
Bounty can kill;
as careless love can kill.

Pharos
(Stonington)

Winter, when the trees are thin and drear,
a finger-touch of light sweeps frosted pane.
Ages, long gone, by the Canopic Nile
the first great Pharos beckoned into port
triremes of black-bearded adventurers
from Ionian isles, or the red-hued
Phoenician sea-tramps with their slaves and loot.

Are things so different in this Yankee port?
We too have traders with their goods and guile.
Our stout lads have traversed many seas.
Here our own Pharos of granite block,
with its own signature, has called by night
to vessels homing from Antarctic shores;
out-reaching through the sea-gloom silently
to pierce the creeping murk of northern fog,
spelling: Night comes on. Come in. Come home.
give over wandering for the day is done.

It started not two hundred years gone by,
from this small harbor and its rocky point.

Small craft unwinding endless ocean trails
came in with foreign wonders on their lips
and cargoes of whale-oil and pelts of seal.
Thereafter, the great four-masters plowed the Sound,
lords in their time of the coastal waters,
where steadfast lights unfailing marked the way;
Corn Field, Sea Flower signalled in the west
and, where the sound pours fiercely to the sea,
salty, deepthroated Race Rock added voice.

Bartlet picked up the sign, Watch Hill and Napatree
talked together in the night, constant guardians.

Though sealers now are gone and schooner hulks
lie dismantled, abandoned by old docks;
draggers at fall of dusk push stoutly home,
trailing their cloud of gulls, most business-like
to shove their noses into waiting berths.
The lights still flash. The small erratic bells
talk to their buoys. Tide stakes lean. Quiet sea-voices
speak up on every hand to meet the fog.

Never mind pharos gone, the Yankees gone,
the schooners grounded.

I need these lights,
the sounds, the rank smell of kelpy reefs.
There's more to it than traders. The sea must speak.
My stream of life draws to the level sea,
where ocean strokes the continental shores
or meets in wild contentions, breast to breast,
never released from conflicts never won.
Free me from the intrusions of mountains,
for sight and sound and saline taste of sea.
I crave its open sky and spread of stars.
I must know by night the silent interviews
of many lights and the fog-horns droning.
By day the tidal marshes my delight,
where intrusive fingers of waters flow
and ebb, changing the patterns of grasses,
bringing the rank fragrance of the mud flats
or drifting kiss of unobtrusive fogs.

There is no ocean conquest save by art.
No man has fenced this sea, possessed its strength,

plowed its shifting acres, put it for sale.
Here's creation, immutable and slow,
impersonal, not too loving, always true,
where harassed souls, forsaken and forlorn,
can cast their earth-bound cares on generous breast.
Since life crawled up creations troubled beach,
the constant comforting of bell and beacon,
with healing stroke of wave and scent of sea,
has calmed the turmoil of our land-locked lives,
where Pharos, reaching through the dark of night,
cries out to wandering souls: Come in. Come home.

Hylas

South wind has pelted the winter pasture,
stale frost in a cloud blows over the hill.
Unlocked from the mud in cattail swamp
the improvident, million-throated peepers
fill the air with their incessant shrilling:
Hylas! Hylas! Hylas! Where is he,
where is the lost comrade of Hercules?

This rocky pasture and this icy swamp
are far from the bright island of Kios,
many a thousand year and mile from there,
and Hercules is numbered with the dead,
and dead the cruel goading of his curse
which drove the Greek islanders, high kirtled,
tramping through pungent thyme-scented pastures
or down cool dells beside the springs,
shouting together the name of Hylas.

Where is Hylas, the nymph-enchanted boy?
Hylas! Hylas! Hylas! — gone forever.
One who stood too long by the mountain pools
charmed by the sleek flanks of the easy-swimming,
green-eyed, lily-breasted water-breathers.

Here our only Hercules is winter,
impotent winter, old and obstinate,
and there's none of us here would stir his legs
on a fool's errand. There is no Hylas,
no Hercules, no boy Hylas. And yet
when April moon rolls out of the dusk
and swims across the silent pool of night,

we stand at the door. Children in their beds
turn, baiting their gentle breaths to listen,
or tiptoe out upon the moon-bright floor
and press small noses to the window pane,
hearkening to the chorus from the swamp.

Diana's delicate fingers have touched
and stirred memories in the uncurling things,
roots of the grasses and the fronded ferns,
whereunder innumerable popping eyes
stare and glitter with her strange enchantments.

Thousands of bubbly throats distended
are shrilling the unknown name of Hylas, —
Hylas! Hylas! Hylas! Where is he,
who once upon a time, under the moon,
when nymphs were abroad, strayed from Hercules.

II

Variable Music

The Crux

Man bravely straddles world,
one foot firmly on the dock,
one on adventuring boat.
A voice upraised for peace on earth,
a fist for freedom's choice.
He cries in constant pain:
Wake up, good dock. Try moving once,
and: Why so fast, brave boat?
Alas, poor crotch!

Warrior

The warrior Socrates,
citizen of the Polis,
drawing his final sword
against stupidity—
reached for the hemlock.

New Planet

Rejoice brave spacemen.
Beneath God's footstool
your billion dollar shit
revolves immortal
in the frigid void.

Style of Man

Style is the signature
of chancy genes,
free of will and mind,
impossible to evoke.
The sweep of hand,
a tone of voice,
all given, never earned,
call the tune
unique to every man.

Bread

Pondering a Foundation Executive,
I wondered if his careful morality
and priestly ambience were really
necessary?
Yet it must take a deal of piety
to turn a whore into a vestal virgin.

Threes

Three fallen leaves chase
madly down the street.
Three eagles whistle and close
high in the blue.
Three raunchy dolphins
caper in one wave.
Three desperate souls
play at odd-man out.
Must everything resolve itself to two?

The Artist

For that foolhardy innocent, the artist,
it's always dawn, always what next.
Mud underfoot, the slash of wilderness,
serpents draining across his path,
voices proclaiming doom, only excite
his childish wonder. Make way. Let him pass.

Altar Piece

Says Shaman to the witch
as his white goddess
came hipping down the aisle,
her lovely eyes aslant
above Mona Lisa smile:
"Do you take me for your man,
now and forever, only me?"
"As you," says she, "take me,
your witch, your wife, for life,
Cling to me close,
as I to you, each to other."

She meets his probing gaze
with soft unfocused eye.
Hands clasp before the priest.
"I do. I will," says each.
What will, what do, remains,
a dance to dance, a pattern spun,
till death do them unite.

Advice to the Lovelorn

The hippopotamus and unicorn
equally are moved by lust and love.
Try to remember, if you are one or other,
the kind of creature you were born
and not turn on until you've found another.

Susanna and the Boys

Crowding together
they part the rushes
where, knee-deep in waters
strides naked Susanna.
Strong arms lift up dark mane,
Round belly arches
above its grotto.
Pillars of thighs
support great buttocks.
They gaze askance at forested armpits.
"So much hair in so many places!
Her legs could crush one," they cry.
Raising their eyebrows, they skip away.

To Her Belly

I know what's lurking
within that lovely pasture,
small chromosomes,
eyes over edge of their fans,
watching and waiting.

Shall I send in pell-mell
the swimmers, the pursuers?

Lechery

Lechery is a name for fun,
as natural as drinking from a spring.
Be sure the shimmering face and form
are not mistook for love.

Winner Take All

Caught with necessity of lust,
tooth and nail and brutal thrust;
in clutch of victory or defeat,
two strangers strew the battle sheet.

Take Care

Who can stand bare
to sensation's avalanche?
Cherish illusions.
The ones you come to believe
flower as truth.
Look well to your own creation.
Only God stands naked to the battle.

Resolution

Each New Year, as I turn the unwritten page,
I vow no more to think about my age.
Allow myself each day but one deplore
and pray to God. Help me to listen more.

Easy Does It

When very young
I learned to run.
At middle age
I built a cage.
And, like a squirrel,
spun in a whirl.

One day I saw
what I headed for
was Marble Town.

I slowed me down.

Panic

Why are we slowing down?
Is this really the station?
Do I have to get off?
I don't wish to settle here.
This is not my home.
Why does the whistle keep blowing?
Can't somebody shut the door?
Where's the conductor?

Once a Man, Twice a Boy

Grandpa chopped a Dryad from a tree,
or so he said.
And she made grateful love to him right there.
He sprang up ten years younger for his fee.
How many times did Grandpa serve this wench,
that now he's like a happy child at knee?

The Charlatan

Sometimes I watch myself in blank amaze
playing both street-musician and his ape,
Needing to hold some stranger's wandering gaze,
I doff my cap, grimace and swirl my cape.
I feel I am not I until I see
myself reflected in some other eye,
then, pocketing the charlatan's quick fee,
am happy there are other tricks to try.

Flatter, but slantingly; tease, but not too much.
Shock and seduce a little, it's getting late.
Suggest, some day just two of us for lunch.
Take down the brand new number. Clinch the date.
"Nice chap," they'll say. "So well informed, so gay."
How better kill another empty day?

I Presume

I presume the mole,
with ultra-sensitive snout,
feels safer tunnelling the dark.
I presume the hunger-maddened termite
dares anything but meet the sun.

I presume the academic fellow
hides in catacombs of mind,
labelling and shelving the bones of life,
lest he shrivel in the light.

Yes

Open—now shut—
eyes—lips—yes.
Move a little.
Be still. Be still.
Is it love,
lust, lechery
or sweet delight?
Yes.

The Reckoning

God save us from sacrificers.
Those humble servants,
when least expected,
bill in hand,
will knock upon the door.

Irony

Irony is the joke we share with God,
crying: Father, how deftly
you pull out the rug.

The Dark of Hours

How often in the dark of hours,
down from habitual tower,
the toll of time drifts by our street.
One, two and three and four, and then,
while the confident ear attends,
there is no following stroke. Suspended,
we wait for news of creeping dawn.

Time comes the full twelve shall strike,
and dark continue without hope of sound.
Shall we still hark for declaration
of the longed-for note; seek, as now,
fulfillment of the promised stroke?

Brave Lads All

From high sanctuary
silent insects glide,
their lethal eggs
scatter the mermidons
in spurts of lovely flame.
Well done, brave lads.
Or, may be,
medium or rare.

Aftermath

Mole wonders what's astir,
tiny emmets seek the air.
The penguins all confer
deep in Antarctic lair.
The last sea-breathing whale
flaunts his great tail.
"Pass the good word," they say.
"Man's done himself away."

III

The Haunt of Time

Even the Greenest

Even the greenest everlasting pine,
wrenched by autumn blast,
casts down the brown
where waiting earth provides new pattern.
So dark sorrow and the stab of grief,
under the green
at doors of death,
seek new harmonies.

The Haunt of Time

In the beginning was neither word nor man.
It began with I remember how it felt,
a window curtain waving in the wind
with summer smells and sounds of no-name,
voices in and out of horizons of dreams;
the variable music of the senses,
the comfort or the want of reaching hands;
nor you nor I nor he, nor tick of time.
Tender breasts reach down to give us suck,
strong arms encircle and a voice is near.
To breathe, to be, to lie beneath the sun
holds all delight, for we are not.
Time is yet quality and has no measure.

What force,
creates desire, stales yesterday's good pleasure,
winds up the clock, gives time first measure,
explodes necessitous iron of the will
and proclaims man? Who asked for this?
What child-mind first said God? What blaze of need,
wrenched to focus in the glass of brain,
aroused this haunt that never can be snuffed?
Spurning dimension of the animal world,
what first led man to stare down the abyss,
in soul's name goaded the innocent beast,
with echo of time madness at his back,
his nerves at pluck, his senses unrequite,
gave shadow to the hawk, gave voice to hound?

Far from the tumult and the bruit of hours
a finger-touch upon an upturned brow
stills every nerve, releases every sense
and we are, as in the beginning, one
with time. Home again to that still center
where search awaits the cry, and the voice prepares.

4 A.M.

Star in the east,
star in the west,
star out the window,
star in my breast,
how many light-years
away do you live?
Are you reaching for Man?
Have you something to give?
Star of no name,
Venus is burning,
Lucifer fades.
Do you tremble with life?
Have you rivers and glades,
calm oceans, soft skies?
Do you see me from there,
straight through my window
where staring I lie?

Let me warn you,
man is a spoiler.
In terror he plunders,
in panic he slays.
If you dare, come swiftly
and soon to our aid.
Never mind wonders,
loving-kindness will do.
I hold your bright image
fast in my sight.
If you're ready, I'm ready.
Try me some night.

Mandala

The artist's single eye,
right in the middle of his forehead,
makes the general focus all his own;
brings universal into singular,
special meaning to the common-place,
shapes every sense,
'til scattered glories rush to focus.
One eye, that dances with the dancers,
spins with the spinners,
'til tongue forgets its venom
and the heart is lost in song.

Symposium

Epicurus:

By god Apollo, little Leontion,
I am tumultuous with joy.
Your letter brought your lovely voice
to fill my thirsty mind.
Thin fare and crust are feast enough
if you pour out the wine.
I see you walk these paths once more
beneath the tent of sky,
lost in sweet thought, your little feet
kick out from robes of white.
Come, or I'll cast a Thracian spell
and thrice spin round and round.

Leontion:

Spell-bound by your bearded words,
I'll soon be by your side.
As one, we'll lick the honeyed bread
and share your Samian wine.
I'll catch my hands within your beard,
while summer lightnings of your wit
caress my eager mind.
Then, pacing through the gardens,
beneath some sheltering pine,
we'll spread our robes upon the ground,
where grows the fragrant thyme,
and round your upright, rugged sides
my silken limbs will twine,
until, though prone and captive,
you shall spin thrice around.

Epicurus

Epicurus walking his garden —
dead two thousand years gone by —
Ignored ambitious snobs who strove
to prove their immortality.
Opposing Love to sterile Law,
he still lives on to save his own
from Plato and theology.

What Went Wrong?

Odysseus, wild wanderer,
did you lose your nerve?
Did mad heart master iron will
to bind adventurous soul to mast?
After Circe, was there nothing left
to charm the Siren from her slippery rock?
No magic, piratical word,
no possible touch, or stab of sudden glance,
to bring that wild one to the master's hand?

Address Book

I sit in the house about to be sold,
I sit in the skin about to drop off.
I pick up from the dust an address book.
One more decision, what to keep, what to take,
what to leave, what to wipe off the slate.

It begins with A, of course, for lovely Anne,
once mine, then married to some no-account.
This was years gone by, what could have happened?
This old address no longer can hold true.
And so on down the alphabet of time.
Why should brave souls come suddenly on death?
And here, if only I had spoken out.
Another, self-defeating, now long gone.
Likker took those most delicately made.
And these two held by love, yet strayed apart.
My God, I sit here where my parents sat,
where toll of years dissolved their earlier lives.
Did they, as now I do, turn towards the young
and wonder, as I do, what ties ring true?
In blindness of youth, these older lives
all seemed one age — call it parent age —
as I remember neither young nor old.
But as they died, inattention lifted
and suddenly old pictures came to mind,
long gone accommodations of the heart.
I heard my mother sing, combing her hair,
dark hair cascading from her bended neck,
and saw my father striding home from work
calling her name, as he flung wide the door.
The skin of years sloughs off. Departing joys,

old companionships, forgotten tokens
of love and friendship race across the page,
now largely cancellations. I said,
I'll just consolidate — cut my heart to bits —
for all the oversights, blind haste, neglect,
toll of stupidities and slippery time,
since the world was young and we all drank wine.

Invisible Sir

Invisible Sir, do I see you yawn,
lifting your garments of rose and pearl
over the mountains of the eastern sky?
One day more?

Do not despair of us!
Reach down again to grasp the faltering hand,
forget the mongrel noise of incantations,
be patient with slaughter, envy, greed
of beasts emerging slowly into light.

We two, who only live through belief, shall live,
recreated and once more enthroned.
Remember, when you first spun this small globe,
rejoicing together we drew in our breath?

Invisible Sir, just one more finger touch
and we can still renew our mutual self.
Together You and undiscovered man,
Invisible Sir, shall make each other whole.

Interview

Lucifer:
I've been up and down among thy people
Lord. You last spoke with me when foolish Job
was scapegoat to your imperial pride.
Why not ask me now, once your right hand man,
then fallen angel: "What of my people?
Does it still go well with them below?"

Lord:
I was about to call the earth thing off,
a bad creation that somehow failed to hatch.
Now, since the fiery secret of the sun
is in their grasp, I'm inclined to let them
bring the whole damned thing about their ears.

Lucifer:
You always were arrogant in failure.
This long sabbatical of Seventh Day
has been a burden more than they can bear.
Why did you quit? Just to watch them struggle?
Are you no better than a mousing Cat?

Lord:
Outcast, guard your tongue. Can you never learn?

Lucifer:
Nothing to lose, Lord. Nothing you can do.
I'm quite ready to share your creature's fate.
All you can do is wipe us off the map
and then where are you, with no servants left?

Lord:
True, but I could start again.

Lucifer:
And botch it again.

Lord:
Perhaps send Jesus back a second time?

Lucifer:
They have no faith. They would not know him now.
Abraham was no lesson. They think him mad,
and Job they hold a masochistic fool,
and as for you, Lord, millions in your name
slaughter each other to bring peace on earth.
You drive your people crazy.

Lord:
It's you who drive them mad. It's a famous fact.

Lucifer:
The Devil it is. They do it in your name
because they've lost the sense of what you are.
Never mind Jesus. It's time you came yourself.

Lord:
I'm busy oiling other cosmic gears.
The incense from the earth grows very faint.
Other worlds await the creative touch.

Lucifer:
Sire, they sent me here to rouse you again.
They trust me as one who understands them.
Tell Him to listen well, is what they said,
for this is truly his last chance on earth.
Tell Him he stands accused of gross neglect.

Lord:
You heard. As I once gave you Job for proof,
I give you all my creatures down on earth.
As I recall there was much splendor in them.

They stand up well against their adverse fate.
Let's see what *you* can do.

Lucifer:
I know my limitations. Answer me,
why did you create their flesh in beauty,
endow them with grace, stir their hungry minds
with godlike aspirations in your name,
then let flesh rot, mind turn to idiocy,
just as perfection neared? A sorry joke,
to raise up hope only in irony.
In a word, treat them like so many Jobs.

Lord:
I told you I am busy. Go your way.

Lucifer:
I shall tell Thy people, Lord—my people—:
"God stands corrupted by his own creation.
He lacks in faith. He leaves it up to you.
There is no hope that He will save your world,
no chance that all those promises are real.
No way to know that change will save the day.
For better or for worse you stand alone,
your weapon love, your strength simplicity.
The best part of himself inheres in you.
As always, I shall be at your left hand
to point the idiot path you still can take.
God looks away. Perhaps you are fortunate.
No longer servile puppets in the dark
but children of the light, now on your own,
yourselves can recreate a godlike god."

Patzcuaro

Through gilded doors ajar,
far down long aisles,
magnificent stands the Virgin;
royal and stiff with azure tile,
a proud Castilian,
bold-breasted, arrogant,
in audience for annunciations.

An unseen hand touches my heart.
Here by shadowy door
weighing on shepherd's staff,
the cares of the world call out
from one, small, carven Man.
His tattered cape
falls from shoulder bones.
A draggle of hair, thorns
aslant, rust-red with blood,
frame the sad brow. Eyes
dark with fatigue of soul,
lost in their own Golgotha,
look me through.
"Brother, I whisper, Brother,
it's a long road.
Rest on your staff. Night comes apace."

The mother does not see
her King of Kings, and He
cannot be bothered,
his thin lips torn
with the everlasting cry:
"Father! Father! Why?"

Kairos
Let Time Stand Still

Lost from this garden centered in my being,
pacing my life to strange, compulsive gods,
one time, full circle home, I came to stop
and found myself helping a daughter born.
Poor, sponge-rubber dumpling in my hands
from surge of blood and water of the womb
raising her little fists, gasping for air.

Watching amazed, I bowed my neck in prayer.
Was not this new life, small part, still my own?
What more could I give to shape her being?
This hope: that as she flowered into woman
forever she remain a child of Kairos.
That this mysterious journey set upon
would hold her central in ambient time,
never slave to metronomic whip
of cruel Chronos, and his measured line
of empty conquests.

Earthbound, in a beginning sensuent world,
once upon a season, unfolding like a rose,
your strong, well-fashioned little body
spilled out deliciously atop the sheets
because, until fresh linen had been brought,
once bathed, you would not occupy your bed.
Your body knew good answers of the flesh.
No clock been struck. No goal been set. Kairos
held you captive in its world of sense,
all one as is a meadow stream of waters,
or summer's sail mastering open seas,
not yet shadowed by the hawk of hours,
no hounds of Chronos snapping at your heels.

Alas, I knew you still must face the test
of purgatory, where death so well disguised,
invites our wayward life to fall in step,
accepting safety from the stamp of same,
one destination, one stomp of many feet,
young faces drained of individual life
marching to drum-beat of a single Will.

Yet all we need lies circled around self,
harmony of sense, instincts, servant mind,
all captive to instant revelation
centered in Kairos with the gift of peace.

Stand naked on creation's mid-night shore,
pick up the great horn-spoon of plenty,
cream-off the silver of the moon-blanched sea
and spill it on your daily porridge.
Stand firm, my love, well nourished in the gifts
dowered at birth on every living soul.
Here at hand is plenty round-about.
Your realm is like a fertile woodland lake,
governed recurrently by sun and moon.
Nowhere, is the name for straight-away,
all you will ever need lies to your hand.

The circle is man's conquest of his Will,
the never ending measure of what is.
The garden without walls, nature at now,
the grasp of hands, voices in communion.
Man needs no journeys to the far away,
no tree of knowledge, the fruit is free,
the mystery revealed with every breath,
unfolding like a red-rose into being,
petal by petal opening, until,
allotted course now run, heart stops its beat.

And I still pray, that here in womanhood
as you in turn bare children to the sun,
you and your blood's dark magic,
complete the flowering you set upon
as child of Kairos, mistress of ambient time,
defiant of cruel Chronos' measured line
of empty conquests that only craze the mind.
Study, my love, to daunt that purgatory
thrust on you by assault of crowding years.
Eternity and future are not one
and when so used end in empty sameness—
Sameness is another name for death—
Recurrent, deviant revelation
is the only language that can speak to life.
All progressions live within our loins,
seeking creative partnership 'gainst death.
The dance of chromosomes within the womb,
minute, disparate, marked for miracle,
uniquely promise, in their helix flight,
the never-before that spells eternity.

I have put down your picture as a child
and confront you as a woman, vital, strong,
still spontaneous with quality of life.
Your knowing hands still heal, nor have forgot
life answers only to art, not conquest.
Life is a bold defiance all the way
and Kairos the only pasture for the heart.
There small courages burgeon into joy
and freedom flowers from discipline of love.

Kairos is an honest pagan word
that speaks eternity when time stands still;
for children, lovers, valiant souls—their birthright.

Children in the Attic

They blow with the wind, scatter in the sun,
but let clouds gather, shaking down the rain
they steal away quietly, one by one,
up the stairs to their secret world again.
From the disordered attic wilderness
of dusty treasure and dim louver-light
you can catch their muffled scuttle as they dress
in crazy garments, hysteric with delight.
Sounds and pregnant silence from the attic
hold the listening downstairs world at mock,
as they resurrect the discards and then panic
their small, irreverent minds with wicked talk.
Call on these wayward children when you can
to rectify the sanity of man.

Not Much

I don't ask much,
just quietly, without talk,
to be where you are.
I like to watch you smile,
drink in your good voice,
see you cross a room.
I don't ask much,
just a finger-touch,
a curious glance.
So little, except—
I mean to have it all.

Friendship

A friend is someone you can swallow whole,
no contract, no accounting can be asked;
no other discipline but love's control,
once given, the chips are down, the die is cast.
Strong beyond addition of one and one,
it is the very flower of life's art.
Though fully joined the task is never done,
and once engaged, never again to part.

Friendship is no common state of man,
plucked from acquaintance by a casual hand.
It is the fruit of need, no conscious plan.
Savoured at random, never at command.
Friendship heals whatever's halt or blind
within the faltering heart or doubting mind.

Love

You talk of love,
do you want me on leash?
You talk of love
always in reach.
Is the habit so dear?
Is possession all?

Let us love at arm's length,
each to his pasture of quiet,
to each his wild retreat,
then homeward turn-about,
lightfoot with heart's desire.

Little Hawk

Little hawk, little hawk,
Come down, sweep down
from high helix.
Come to my wrist,
no hood for eyes,
no chain for talon.
Little hawk, little hawk,
the falconer calls
and bares his wrist.

Johanna

They tell me Johanna is gone —
a light snuffed out. Not so.
I heard the joy of her voice,
saw the pride of her youth.
Walking the long Aegean strand,
her arms picked up the sun,
small sands leaped beneath her feet.

Honoring such life we shall stand
erect and stare down death,
until, in our own time,
at the end of the long walk,
there, pacing the same white beach
by the blue sea, we greet Johanna
drawing near in the light.

My Name

When she spoke my name
it aimed at sharing,
of light and dark,
of walking the sun,
waiting out the cloud.

Calling my name
she wrapped me in her love.
Then was gone.
Never again at my side
to challenge, as her right,
never again to say yes,
as was her right.

Touching my name,
she disappeared.

I Beg to Report

We who are left gaze out upon the sea,
grey, impersonal, soft-enfolding sea,
beyond whose gates no answer ever comes.
The waves that danced for you now bend their heads.
The erratic, gentle bells at harbor mouth
answer each other as they always have,
marking the last sound you could have heard
when the sea you loved took your final breath.

So long as I live you shall not have died.
From our long marriage I shall choose good gifts
sprung from the bounty of your generous heart,
recalling your courage and your reckless love.
The mind plays many tricks, the heart beats true.
My mind raced desperately in cage of skull,
wrenched at its prison bars and wildly cried
impossible questions. Death did not hear.
Death means no second chance. I cling to life
where all of hell and heaven lies at hand.

Strength flowers from the dung-hill of despair,
whence the terrible dreams that liberate,
as you thrice tried to reach me in the night.
First, in horror, your dead, averted face
passed by me as I called. Later, at home,
young in the sunlight, you set the table.
"Children," I whispered, "be gentle, she's back."
"Just for now," you said, "They're coming for me."
"Not so," I cried. "We'll kill them, every one."
And last, I dreamed the door flung open wide,
you stood there bright with love, saying: "Beloved,
I'm home again. It's all a bad mistake."

Though heart bleed and the cruel knife still turns,
I shall not let our conjoined life go stale.
Why should all we shared fade into dream?
Is death new life, no life, or mirrored image,
where all our former good companionship,
the mutual struggles and the sudden joys,
stay neutralized? I will not have it so,
or lose forever the feel and tug
of that good journey we set foot upon.
We had each other and our hearts were high.
Having each other we were unafraid,
armored in innocence, eager to face
and force the gateways of a wilderness.
We found the fiercest demons lurked within.
Why deny perverse and difficult hours
when love reverses into cruel hurt?
What hostages we give accepting love,
vulnerable and naked to the flung word
stupidly uttered, slashing the heart!
Two quiet souls at sword's point stand at bay.
Amazed, suddenly from each other's eyes
read strange hostility. Can this be us?
Persisting, somehow we weathered out those squalls
and forced our varient passions to one course.
Good hap, my love, the fierce interludes
bound me more strongly to you in the end.

Of all the myriad dances ever danced,
for better or for worse, our dance is done.
Now life's fountain tumbles back to earth,
the music muted and our sharing done.
The flowering time gone by, the sun rides on,
I still hold out my empty arms wide-spread,
harking vainly to have you call my name

and feel again your small, strong hand in mine.
Though mind demands of life it still survive
perpetuating its unique design,
that death but punctuates the fall of seed,
the springing of the flower; life says No.
There is no promise of a second chance.
Life is a larceny from the dark unknown,
snatched between the prime and set of sun.
Love and comradeship are vagrant gifts
that must be tended with a constant hand.
Nothing remains the same in sequent time,
no man, nor beast, nor any greening thing.
The globe itself can be a star put out,
swept up in vapour of lost galaxy.
Though seed and cosmos may renew themselves,
the self-same man is never recreate.
So I shall cherish your bright passage,
no questions asked, fed by no false hope
that your dear image linger in the glass.

I beg to report, little giant, my own,
who with me built reality from dream,
things that you tended, by your love persist.
Your children grow and thrive and stand up straight.
Your husband wears the garment of your care,
lies down at dusk within your tended home,
for better or for worse, once more to dream.
Each familiar season as of old
answers the compulsion of its life.
The harbor bells still sound, rain sweeps the sea,
tides breathe gently, earth burgeons, the same sun
rolls on. The drum-beat of the coursing blood
drives man and woman into waiting arms.
The fire-folk glisten in the mane of night.

Your garden grows. Springtime trees shake out
their lovely crowns, inviting oriole.
Flowers raise their faces, expecting the same touch
as when you kneeled to them in tender care.
I see you walk the town, quick step, head high,
shouldering oars, straight to your small boat.
People look up as if to call your name.
This always and so much more remains.
I shall not stoop to the waters of Lethe,
pretending another dream can mend my life.
Each to his own self tune must see it through.
I cling to familiar, dumb, intimate things,
all once at home to our mutual touch.
Beyond self-pity, let me now recall
how we two drank the salt, sea air, turned home,
set the board and tasted bread and wine.
Or how you flung back curtains of the dawn,
inviting flood of sun and conjured joy.
Though my heart bleed, let me ever hear
the step of your lively feet about our house;
the echo of your voice, calling my name
will keep alive our long companionship.

So I beg to report, around your house
this May the Johnny-jump-ups raised their heads
turning this and that way in the sun.
Narcissus you transplanted from the Farm,
prospered as if your tending hands were there.
Your garden, could it speak, would ask me: "Where?"
Now it is fall and you have been gone a year.
There is a rain of bright leaves, though no wind blows.
Farewell, my one true love, fare you well
Into that long sleep and no more sorrow.

Confident Against My Shoulder

Two gulls weave by,
one in pursuit plaintively calling.
Two sparrows dive from the eaves,
always, one in pursuit.
I dreamed I walked the beach.
Brilliant with life, you came running,
took my arm. I whispered:
"Where have you been this time?
It's been so long?"
"Never mind," you said,
"Here we are at last."

I awoke, no head resting
confident against my shoulder.
A cock crowed. A dog barked, somewhere.

Skip Stone

The first infant cry,
flip of flung stone
meeting first wave
of the cold sea.
Skipping stone
spills energy
from wave to wave,
slower, slower,
to final, gentle
folding of waters.
Another stone,
faster, slower, gone.

If Only

'If only' is a self-deceiving cry
conjuring up impossible virtues
to perpetuate the poison cup of grief.
If only I had offered while she lived
perfect subtleties of attention,
never missed a trick of sympathy,
read every thought, anticipated
every need. Then what?
Would that truly be love,
or impossible tenderness
breeding the curse of perfection,
boredom and death of love?

A Rainy Day

i

All day by the dying fire
a hood of darkness drowns my sense—
white hawk slashes winter gloom—
and I have died a death.

Touch of friends,
alas, those few that live,
gone. What bourne is this?
No trace of trail,
no sign, no golden word.
Wrapped in wan-hope
how shall I greet the sun?
No help at hand, no second chance.
Is this the only race I run?

I do not want to go.
I choose this sad world.
I long after more.
My voice has not been heard.
Is no one at the door?

ii

We walk the coals of fire,
all Macedonians of fate,
sustained by love or faith,
blind to disaster.

Pulsing rivers of blood
cry answer to the sun's flame
One great conflagration
creating life, blasting constellations.
All one variously-timed
magnificent: Yes.

A rock in space becomes a comet.
Articulate man,
sensient nerve-end
of the cosmic dance,
takes God's hand.
Speaks to the mystery.

So we burn our moment through the dark,
in one door and out another.
Gird to walk the coals. It has been done.

Hark to the Piper

Let no man walk backward towards the grave,
with eyes inverted, counting empty days
stale as the foam of a receding wave —
The bag-pipe over the hill still plays,
evoking valiant life. Each man's self tune
picks up the drone of heart, the chanter breath,
that chromosome first danced to in the womb,
a challenge each must follow unto death.

How various our venturous footsteps seem,
how bold the choice of self-willed enterprize,
or, strangely victims of a pin-ball game,
we lost the way and never seized the prize.
Hark for the piper whose seductive beat
and single music ever guides our feet.

On the Square

The lean old man,
hard as a hickory limb,
sits on the square,
soaks up the noonday sun.
The roots of desire
twist in his heart,
alert to the arrogant flaunt
of beauty on the march.
Must he sit content,
sifting his memories?
He snaps his fingers
for another glass.

Passage

Do not ask that you remain you.
Here, yes. Hereafter, no. But
something of you will rub off,
like, but not, you.
Small streams, uniquely self,
flow into rivers and they,
less like themselves,
draw to the universal sea.
Even that sea is slave to the sun,
rises in and out of storms,
transformed rains down on earth.
Again small streams
no sameness ever in their new beginnings,
sing and leap in the highland pastures
and for a while, not long,
leave individual mark.

Recording

Present fades into dream,
slippery as wind on waters
the future sweeps upon us,
for an instant stopping time,
as a swallow touches still-pond
on the wing.

As If

To work and live as though immortal.
To stare down the abyss and be at home,
mastering the terror and despair,
saving your tears for accidents of love.
Bet your life on dignity and pride,
as if immortal, as if immortal.

R.G.

Embattled innocent,
ghost-raddled lion;
far-ranging mind
engined by Eros.
Scholar, Poet.

The Pipes

What wild soul
first plucked the reed,
squeezed the breath of life
from belly of a sheep?
The pipes of combat
prove life and death
one. Love and death, they cry,
one dance, one dauntless tune
defying blank hereafter.

End Music

The cup I dip comes leaking from the well.
I've seen these sights I see a thousand times,
and all the scents and sounds along the way.
I've messed around the by-ways here too long.

Everyone knows me. God! and so I them.

I want out. I want to walk right out
and keep on going. Anywhere will do.
Just to bend my footsteps somewhere else
beyond the accustomed houses of this town.
No more town meetings. No more do-good groups.
Get out of uniform, challenge afresh
disordered mind and aimless beat of heart,
with something more than whistling in the dark.

"Ah," they'll say. "He needs to find himself."

I doubt that. Just which self, which I, at last?
I need no dodges to concoct new selves.
I've got a closet full of them at home.
It's here and now I'm after. New wine, new friends.
No more hazy hometown recognitions:
"I've hardly seen you. You must have been away."

Somewhere, I know, there'll be waiting down the path
a bistro and a table in the sun.
Voices will call my name, faces lift up.
With a deep sigh I'll stop and sit me down,
here by the road, glass in hand, waiting to see
if there's not something up I may have missed.
Something I want to know, but don't yet know;
something long expected, about to be.

I hear a few friends hailing starry-eyed—
"It's nothing like you think back there in Time.
It's a brand new feeling, an unwritten page.
You can't describe it."
                                        No? Then let me try.
I've unwound horizons in my day
and never felt at loss. I'll just stay put
and watch the greatest show on earth pass by,
within the realm of music and man's speech,
here, close on stage, a good orchestral seat.
They all are here, Popes, Devils, Fat Indian Yoyos,
angels on vacation, children with their eyes.

In fact, right now beside this singing stream
the self-same earthly things I've talked about.
All is familiar, dogs, donkeys, vineyards
spreading out from farmsteads on the hill.
The mountains keep their distance in the sky.
I even hear the breathing of the sea.
I'll call the waiter for a round for all.

Suddenly, I seem to know each face!
What is this place? I dare not ask the name.

IV

American

Author's Note

The selections that follow have been taken from the narrative epic poems, *Leifsaga* and *West Walking Yankee,* both published in the 1930's and then put together, revised and augmented as *To the End of West,* published in 1970.

When the viking north experienced one of those mysterious and periodic outbursts of energy which come upon a race from time to time and make it supreme for a moment of history, Iceland was a society of vigorous and democratic freemen, minor chieftains who had pulled away from the single rule of Norwegian kings like Olaf Trygvesson. In Iceland a school of story-tellers arose whose duty and pleasure it was to recite the exact history of the life and deeds of its leaders, their heritage, and a scarcely appreciated part of our own. From these first Norse saga-makers we learn of women like Gudrid the Fair, of Eric the Red, who settled Greenland, and of his son Leif the Lucky, chief among the western rovers whose long ships first found the American continent four centuries before Columbus. Men as easy with the open sea as is a cowboy with his western plains.

When Englishmen established the first thin Atlantic frontier within sight and sound of the ocean waters in Elizabethan times, the yankee trail began its sun-drag west. American men and women settled and moved on again in Conestoga wagons, on horseback and on foot, for two centuries, until the surf of the wide Pacific called a halt. A nation of pioneers became a nation of entrepreneurs; exchange and barter became paper credit, speed and mechanization completed the conquest of the West.

The nature of this great migration to the end of west, its immediate effect on the men who pushed it foward into each new dawn of the open trail, and the ultimate effect in creating what is the American character in ourselves; this heritage has been my study in these poems. A search—for whatever conquest there is—a search for self.

H.C.

Gudrid the Fair

Who is this dreaming one,
who casually, with such a queen-like grace,
passed by just now? Her braided hair hangs long,
her arms throw back more light than the sky holds.
Is this a trick of fate, that here at home,
myself, who knows the wonders of the world,
have looked upon a goddess and must die?
For certainly she will be ever walking
lightly over the turf before my eyes,
stately and well-formed beyond all women
my eyes have seen since first they followed women.

Gudrid's
Song of the Warlocks

Hail day! Hail sons of day!
Night, and thy child the moon.
Look thou with gentle eyes this way.
And bring all good things soon.

Hail, all ye gods! Goddesses, hail!
And all the generous earth.
Give us wisdom free from bale,
And healing hands and mirth.

Bring plenty to these folk in hall,
Feed fire both day and night.
To those that spin, good luck befall,
Good name to those that fight.

Mannan, Ran and Lear, ye three,
Who watch where sea-paths wind;
Let the far-wending boats go free,
Till they their harbors find.

If earth go dry, if the dew fail -
Freya, harken to my song -
If beasts moan in the dale,
And fish from the sea are gone;
Send thou warm rain and long;
Spawn the salt sea, malt the ale.

If wanhope and dark despair,
Betray the lone wanderer;
Azir, ye gods of the air,
Save from sudden fear,
Dispel unmanly care,
Heaping laughter on laughter.

All women who wail and weep,
With full breast and empty knee;
Bird of forgetfulness,
Dusk-wending heron, free
With wings, with shadow of wings;
Shroud sorrow in saving sleep.

And all with age oppressed,
Haunted with uselessness,
Dusk-wending heron,
With wings, and the shadow of wings,
Touch with forgetfulness,
Till things are no longer things.

The Death of Olaf

Like storm-bedraggled tern
whose small wings have outridden the wanton gale,
a ship with storm-sail bent to broken oars
made Brattahlid and leaned against the shore.
All neighboring folk foregathered with delight,
when Leif and Eric called them into hall,
and told them Halfred, the Icelandic skald,
first out from Norway on the western sea,
had come with bruit of battle in the east,
and death of Olaf Trygvesson, the King.

In summer of the Thousand year,
The Norse king raised the battle spear,
With the *Long Serpent* to the fore
And three-score fighting vessels more.
Like hissing swans they skim the sea
Towards battle in the south country,
To breast far Baltic shores.

He took the helm of the sweetest craft
That ever walked upon the sea.
He looked at his many men and laughed;
His heart was tight with fearless glee.
The *Serpents, Long* and *Short*, the *Crane,*
Lead off a fleet whose like again
Shall never front this northern world.
The oars bit, the waters swirled,
When Olaf hunted down the Dane.
Opposing from the Danish land,
Long-sided ships slide down the strand,
To ride upon the curling flood
As yet unstained with battle-blood.

In every vik, in every fiord,
Sun wakes light from spear and sword
Of a mighty viking horde,
Manning the wains that plow the sea,
Riding the chargers of the tide.
Men marvelled so many ships could be
With all their ocean wings spread wide.

Against the Norsemen these three lend
Strength one to another, Danish Svend,
Olaf the Swede, Eric the Earl;
These three their battle-flags unfurl
And wait beneath an island shore
With gift of death for one king more.
Off Vendland, west of Rugen isle,
Sigvald, the Jomsberg viking vile,
Pretending friendship with the Norse,
Leads Olaf on a traitor's course:
"King, let the smaller ships sail free,
You and your great ships follow me
Close on keel-track by the strand;
Deep water lies along the land."
The *Serpent* and ten vessels more
Leave the main fleet, skirt the shore.
Rounding Rugen, close on Svold,
King Olaf sees the plot unfold;
Sees, where island shadows drift,
Three fleets waiting under cliff.
Who love the isle-encircling sea;
Who love the sword-storm's gleaming light;
Follow the keel-tracks, follow me,
While Olaf fights his last sea-fight.

Olaf the Swede, Eric and Svend
Stand on the shore; their looks they bend
Across the clear and sparkling sea,

Naming which the ships might be.
"First the *Serpent*," says the Swede,
"By her armament and speed."
But Eric the Earl said: "No, not so.
'Tis Eindrade of Gimsur, let him go."
Then came a larger and more proud.
Says Svend: "King Olaf must be cowed,
His *Serpent* has no figure-head;
Our fleet has filled the king with dread."
"Not yet," says Eric, "not this one,
She belongs to Erling Skialgson;
A deadly vessel, let it sail,
Then he shall be of no avail."

More ships came on well into view,
Each one greater than these two.
Then a large and glancing ship,
Proud with golden dragon prow,
Drew praise from every watcher's lip.
"This," said the Earl, "is Olaf now."
Says Svend: "It shows a noble mind,
To build a ship of such a kind,
So long, so beautiful and sheer.
Here is a ship I mean to steer."
Says Earl Eric to his men,
Rushing to their ships again:
"Svend can save himself much pain,
The *Serpent* shall not fall to Dane
Nor Swede take her while Norsemen can.
Who kills this king must be a man."

Now King Olaf gathered close
His few great ships. "Strike sail," he said,
"And bind our vessels head to head.
Never shall I be one of those
To flee from fight, whatever odds;

Our lives are not our own, but God's.

No man shall ever learn from me,
The whirling weapon-cloud to flee."
He stood high on the quarter-deck,
A golden shield hung round his neck;
A golden helm flashed on his head;
His short fighting cloak was red.
He asked Ulf, the fo'castle chief:
"Who are these nearest, in your belief?"
"These, King, are Danes we first shall fight."
"These Danes are soft. Those on the right?"
"Olaf the Swede, and his array."
"Better," said Olaf, "they should stay
At home and lick their pagan bowls,
Our swords shall reft them of their souls.
What great ship lies the other way?"
"Earl Eric Hakonson, they say."
Says Olaf: "Yonder lies our fight.
Norse Eric is a man of might.
Now blow the battle-horns to board
And let us clear this Danish horde."

King Olaf from his greater craft,
Threw out grapplings fore and aft,
Dragging Dane-boats to his side.
The humming spear, whistling arrow,
Steel-blue sword, bit the marrow
Of many a Dane and the Danes died.
Then Swedish Olaf took Svend's place
And fought his namesake face to face;
But like the Danes, he too gave way
Before the wild Norse battle-play.
Then it came as Olaf said;
Earl Eric, when the kings had fled.

Laid his iron-bearded boat
Where the deadly *Serpents* float.

Said Olaf: "Svend shall learn aright
How it is when Norsemen fight;
Though would I had another score
Of our brave lads that died before.
I see the *Crane* has lost her crew,
And the *Short Serpent*, Nefia's pride,
Spills too much blood upon the tide."
Those left in life made slippery way
To where their brave king stood at bay.
The wounded under benches reel;
Their heads hang down along the keel.
Forward, the fo'castle men go mad,
Unmindful of the sharp blade thrust,
Howling like wolves with berserk lust,
Still in heavy armor clad,
They think themselves on solid ground
and leap the sides, and all are drowned.

Einer Tamberskelve drew taut
His mighty bow and coolly fought.
He sent his arrow close beneath
Earl Eric's helm, like whispering death.
Then Eric called his archer, Finn:
"We must kill Tamberskelve to win."
An arrow with a crackling sound
Split the Norseman's bow right down.
King Olaf heard and turned his head:
"What has broken now?" he said.
"Norway from thy hands, O King."
"Not yet," says Olaf, "while I can fling
This heap of spears. Here, take my bow
And shoot Earl Eric through and through."

Then Einer drew the new bow tight,
Until it split beneath his might:
"Too weak a bow for a mighty king,"
He said, and let the weapon fling,
And drew his sword and laid about.
Then suddenly there came a shout.
Earl Eric leads his men aboard
Where Norsemen fight with broken sword,
With splintered shield. They can not stand
Against Earl Eric's fresh command.

Olaf on quarter-deck alone,
Flickering spear-death showers down
Till spears are gone; then looks along
The *Serpent's* deck, where used to throng
His Drontheim lads. He meets their eyes,
Their frozen grin, their wide dead eyes.
"So be," he said and drew a breath,
And sprang to his deep-sea death.

A drift of corpses on the sea,
Wolf and raven along the shore;
Hard and bitter the decree:
Olaf of Norway is no more.

Death Chant for Eric

Long years since first these eyes saw light,
And a new voice cried in the night;
Young bones, young sinews took delight,
And this man stood in manhood's might.

Now runs the river back to the sea,
Thread spins out at the Norn's decree,
Swift bird from cage of bone goes free—
O harken, ye Azir, hear me.

Let yon dusk-wending heron come
And wing this lonely spirit home.
Let Eric sit with the hero host,
And drink the mead and make his boast.

Let him sit at the Warrior Thing;
Let night, the good herdsman, bring
Old comrades once more to the fire;
Let them drink of fulfilled desire.

To The Western Rovers

Mannan MacLear, lord of the sea,
Njord, who walketh over the wave,
with this good harp against my knee
and silence for the harper's fee—
from the sea's laughter and the hushed lave
of sliding waters in the kelpy cave—
I strike the western rover's stave.

I sing the valiant of the sea;
the tall men of the long sight,
the scattered ships, their windy glee,
reaching beyond the gannet's flight,
winter by winter down the world,
further than the sun is hurled.

Long have I heard the roar and rage
the onslaught of the western sea,
and made the choice and paid the wage
of the lone man whose will is free
to follow the star and bend the oar
that steers from safety and the shore.

Ours the wild mid-ocean flight,
where curtains of the dawn unfold,
and the small sail comes out of night,
bellying bright with slant of gold,
and gliding planks of oak all keep
their time and rhythm with the deep.

Women there be who rock and weep,
smooring fires on deserted hearth,
waiting the long ships that sweep
the wide sea-acres of the earth;

where spindrift and the racing wrack
hide their swiftly fading track.
We, beyond need of woman's breast,
beards by breath of sea winds lifted,
stretch upon the thwarts and rest,
strength by no soft woman sifted;
our eyes meeting the one bright eye
of cold moons walking down their sky.

Our dreams of Tir-nan-og the blest,
shaped on the far horizon cloud,
at the world's edge beyond the west,
where music of the surge is loud,
and every wave is the ninth wave,
and all their luck is on the brave.

By the golden strand at set of sun,
under the wood by the green meadows,
the harper with his harp unslung,
softly over the moon-flecked shallows,
floats his harping, and the mermaids creep
along the reefs and shake off sleep.

The daughters of the Lochlann King
comb their tangled hair and mark
the crying of the plucked harp string,
and strain their green eyes through the dark—
with flash of foam-white limbs they stand
stark and wild upon the strand:

their kisses cool as the cool cress,
arms like the peeled willow wand,
skin softer than the touch of mist;
their singing like the silver sound
of mountainy waters, and their love
a bliss no mortal tongue can prove.

Come, ye western roving men,
take oar and sweep the land farewell;
heave the silver sea, and then
up sail to meet the ocean swell;
our doom the never-ending quest
to find the isles beyond the west.

The Yankee Trail

The boundaries of salt wilderness gave way
to rumor of wild Eden, fabulous,
sprawling the western world,
Atlantis freeing from the dark and deep
of olden legend; the land of new-found hope,
no more impounded by the savage waste
of unknown waters. Golden word took wing
of generous streams, warm sun, bright shores and winds
to breathe thereof was drinking of strong wine.
God's room, they said, to stand erect and swing
the axe of freedom; equal chance for all
to carve inheritance in Paradise.
The continent, a dark mysterious bride,
distant and self-contained, waited the tread
of million-footed, white-skinned ravagers.

One hundred years a scatter of small sail
from Verrazzano to the Admiral Smith,
returning with the subtle gold of dreams,
writ watery names along indifferent shores,
all unaware of many glinting eyes,
the guttural cries, the awe-inspiring tale
of Quetzalcoatl hailing from the East.
Was this the Fair God of the morning star
gliding in with wings of the pearly dawn,
whose laughter was the wind upon the wave,
whose anger spoke from thunder-cloud and struck,
with talons of the lightning? Was this He,
come down the generations of dark minds,
whose plenty-dropping hand, whose peaceful step
would shed new glory on the Indian tribes?

The Eagle of the mountains wheeled on high,
a speck against the burning eye of sun,
his screaming lost upon the western wind.
Cruising the sweep of forest, he sailed forth
above the wrinkled, silver-stretching sea.
With folded wing he hurtled down the air
to dart his cold inspection, to descry
what creatures came intruding on the wild
with whirling axe, with coiling chimney smoke.
And only he could answer how these first
vanished there beneath the rustling green
marking one word, CROATAN, on a tree.
Only the Eagle of the Wilderness would see,
year upon year, the little ships unload
the endless axemen, watch the small boats climb
the tumble and the rush of inland streams,
count many smokes and harken where the trees
trembled and shook their lovely crowns and fell
revealing the new cabin and proud man
casting his golden handfuls.

Walking After Hope

Amen to all this walking after hope
escaping from the devil in the breast.
Here lies my furrow. Here must I plod on
the length of years; but seed of my slow toiling,
these men, my sons, are no more mine to hoard
than corn we spill upon the wilderness.

Conestoga Wagon

I built her with these hands. I made her right.
Three years of seasoning in every plank,
hickory, oak and popple. I ground the paint.
Now ain't that red a beauty, and the blue
shining from these boards like all the sky?
She's long and limber. See her tail perk up—
stylish I calls it, and that cloud of hood
and all the curling iron work.

A Quiet Summer's Night

I seem to see a quiet summer's night
with little owls complaining in the trees
putting an edge to silence. The logs caved in,
the ashes settled with a whispering sound.
The shadowy crests rolled eastward into dawn
and caught the sun and towered clean and clear,
kindling in my mind, with the day's bright fire,
a notion to climb up there and find out
the top of something and stare wide around
across the frozen tumult of these hills.
For our long wandering in the forest dark,
the noontide sun and all the light of day
had been a kind of dimness. When we plunged
over the fallen timbers through the swamps,
under the watery waste of glimmering green,
we struggled as if beneath a weight of sea.
The very air was thick. I was possessed
to climb the tallest trunk its hundred feet
and bathe my drowning senses in clean winds,
drink the blue heaven, stare into the sun
and spur my spirit with a gift of wings.
Thus, from a tree-top on a rising knoll,
once, across the waves of surging green,
the Alleghenies hung in the haze of west
guarding the far unknown.

First Encounter

The frost was on the leaf, the stain of Fall
painted the highlands in a crimson net
when Jesse Scott came riding. The wine-brisk
the golden-drenched, the rich autumnal pause
of the full ripened year cast dreamy spell
on man and beast and hushed the wilderness.
The driven plow-share of his mind running
the sequent acts of men down many years,
now quietly came to halt at furrow's end.
Scanning through the well-remembered ways
of his boyhood and his manhood, a new self
wrote finish. The ceaseless fight and turmoil,
the war with nature and his fellow man
within these mountains, drifted into space,
appearing as a quality of dream.
Once more the answer to the spirit's quest
escaped the definition of his will;
but as a huntsman stalking, time on time
delays the perfect moment of the kill
sure of his final triumph, so Jesse Scott
rode with Ohio ringing in his heart.

The Open Trail

In the far mountains on the beaver grounds
the Free Trappers, the solitary men,
roamed in their pride, kings of the wilderness.
For ten swift years the Rocky Mountain world
was theirs. And then the Conestogas rolled
with hooded white, with sifting turn of wheel
bearing the plowmen and their family yoke
to break the wavering double-rutted trail.
They pierced mirage, they followed after false,
only to mark the unwritten continent
with true discoveries more strange than dreams,
of giant forests, fountains that spouted fire,
canyons so steep and wide their vastness held
the silence of eternity. They found
virgin plunder awaiting strength of arm.

Jed Smith, resolute god-fearing leader
of the godless, in the year of Twenty-seven,
launched his little band of mountain man
out from the Salt Lake upon the endless seas
of dancing desert sand. They the first men
to climb the cold Sierras and come down
under the dark of the Sequoia woods.

They smelt salt winds and heard afar,
louder than whisper of pines, a strange sound.
Some, accustomed only to singing streams,
were stopped in fear at the low, unceasing
rumble and murmur of Pacific shores;
for they had never heard the sea nor seen
its vast and various monotony.
Spurring their horses to the sun-bright plain

they caught, beyond the California green,
the long white seam of beach, the endless haze
of the eternal ocean. They sat them down,
harassed by whistling arrow, by hunger,
by clutch of thirst and brunt of wilderness.
What unholy glee courses in the blood
when their hoofs scatter the scent of valleys
and they eat and fill the cup and hear
small feet coming and sensual laughter.

Now Dawns Begin

Now dawns begin and the arching fall of suns
count the slow measure of the westward creep.
Quiet are the prairies in the uncertain
wash of night's end. A small wind stirs.
  Eastward
a delicate hand creates shape of earth.
A bird sings and slowly the gift of light
washes like new the same world. Bright sunlight
streams upon the enchanted trees, the plain
ripples alive; dogs bark; men rub their eyes;
small hands reach out and slip the dew-wet thongs,
and the devotional and lazy-scented smoke
of breakfast fires ascend from the wagon train.
Round about in the low mists the oxen
heave to their cloven feet and snuff the grass,
studying with mild stupidity new day.
The cry Catch-up, Catch-up, rings through the camp.
Horsemen wheel among the uncertain beasts,
steers groan, mules squeal, men shout and curse
adjusting the tight cinch or heavy yoke.
The leader rides along the restless train:
"Let's go," he yells and the drivers cry:
  "Stretch out."

Spring like a fire has run the prairies,
from the black deep of soil the indigo
and wild pea spangle the onrolling earth.
A door is opened in the hearts of men,
glad for this illimitable room.
The same horizon day by day recedes
before the slow revolve of turning wheel.

Once a small cloud, dark in the hazy west,
suddenly fanned like a great smoke end rolled
across the bright assurance of high noon.
Men battened down the waggons. A jagged cloud
dragging a belly of torrential rain
shattered with swords of light the copper gloom.
Beasts bowed down before the whistling gale.
Time and the mind of man stood still
beneath the streaming rage of element.
Cold and clear was the evening light. Rainbows
shimmered on the bright of plain.
New born, men huddled by the fires at dusk
ready once more to face the endless trail.

Last Word

Bill Scott pressed East unwinding desert miles
until he came to camp by the namesake place
marking the limit of his father's search.
The sun wheeled westward in an empty sky
and sank beneath the mountains.
Came Eagle, says:
"What do you do now, Yankee? What remains?"
"No great thing, just give me time and peace
to rummage through the lumber of my mind;
nothing new, no further place, no prize.
Let me see whole, in one clean lightning stroke
our land that ranges west from sea to sea.
The answer lurks in rocky cave of skull,
all one dimension with a man called Scott."
"Not enough," cries Eagle. "Who is this Scott?
One more Yankee with a restless foot,
or a man, who pacing out the continent,
has long last come to terms with what he is?
How different are you from your buried sires?
What mean the battle-scars of western search?
At rope's end you must read yourself, old man."
"Voice, give me time to see what I can see.
Let me cut through false to the final gift,
to know what is that is at long day's end.
I must know before I die, who's dying."
"Time flies," cried Eagle. "You are not in charge.
The jig is up. In running out your course
you've spurned time's coin in creating what?
Is there a better image of a man?"

Bill Scott sat lost, deep in his world of skull,
revisiting the altars of his life;

many hearth-fires, good fellowship with friends,
the daily sharing of his daily bread.
He caught the sun-drag of the fading light
that pulled himself and sires across the world,
looking for perfection here on earth.
"What goal was in your mind," screamed Eagle.
  "Come!"
The bowed head now no longer could reply.
Words failed. Only the mind kept throbbing on.

Wasn't the search the answer, that enough?
The act of standing up to face down death—
not What, but How—the style of life itself,
the art of sensing the created Thing?
"Speak," urged Eagle, "if you're still alive.
What of these folk, this western-walking horde,
lustful and greedy, without decorum,
rough, brutal and unceremonious;
fierce children, impatient conquerors
haunted by time, blind to their fate,
who drag their bloody feet from place to place.
You, man, are one of them. What is the aim?
What is the expectation of my land?"

No voice reached through. His inner eye now raced
down the long years with instant apprehension.
He saw at last the hopelessness of search
for any answer to the cloud of dream;
he knew full well that there was no escape.
He'd staked his life. Each sire had wagered his,
but not enough.

                    Now he was old and tired
and faced indifferently the stroke of death.
"Awake!" screamed Eagle. "You've not answered me."
Then stalking closer saw an empty corpse,

eyes to the East, head sunk and motionless.
Says Eagle, soaring up on silent wing:
"There has to be another. There must be
someone, somewhere, who can speak my tongue."

Henry Chapin

HENRY CHAPIN "is incurably American," writes Josephine Jacobsen. "Without a line of patriotic rhetoric, deeply and inevitably his poetry rises out of the New England soil." Born in 1893, he grew up in Springfield, Massachusetts, where his pioneer forebears settled in the early 1600's. These origins, despite his wide travels in the world, are implicit in the themes and perceptions of his work.

He began writing and publishing poetry in the 1920's as an expatriate in Europe, but he was eighty before his first collection of shorter poems, *A Celebration,* appeared in book form. Chapin's longevity and his late flowering make it difficult to realize that he and his friend, F. Scott Fitzgerald, America's "spokesman" of the twenties, are in fact contemporaries and graduated from Princeton the same year.

Chapin's literary output in the 1930's and 1940's was largely subordinated to an active political life and farming in Bucks County, Pennsylvania, though he produced three notable epics of western migration in this period: *The Adventures of Johnny Appleseed,* 1930; and the two historical narrative poems *Leifsaga,* 1934; and *West Walking Yankee,* 1940.

Not until about 1960, when most of his contemporaries were drawing retirement benefits, did Chapin turn his full energies to writing, and to poetry in particular. It is perhaps no coincidence that in the same period he returned to his native New England—with his wife the late Paula Van Dyke—to live in Stonington, Connecticut. Nine books published in the last two decades are testimony to that late outburst of literary energy.

The present volume comprises a range of his work—from *New England Sentiment,* published in the *London Mercury* in 1926, brief selections from his historical sagas of the 1930's, and the larger body of late work, represented by such new poems as *Li Po Comes Home,* written last year.

In 1980 he moved to Peterborough, New Hampshire, where he had previously spent several seasons as a fellow at the MacDowell Colony.